VOICES
SELDOM HEARD

Tom Everett

Poetry by

TOM EVERETT

DEDICATION

To Shirley,
Susan and Matthew,
And Riley,
With Dearest Love

Tom Everett became the Director of the Baptist Center at Western Heights Projects in Knoxville, Tennessee on March 5, 1975.

That was a different time.

Gerald Ford was the President of the United States.

Bill Battle was UT's Head Football Coach.

Saigon had not yet fallen.

And Elvis really was still alive.

CONTENTS

1. SUNDERED EXODUS

Some 1950's Appalachians
 Hunting work paying
Good wages
Went north, and further.

Three uncles went to
Detroit, Chicago and Afghanistan,
To work at Packard, as tailor,
Heavy equipment operator.

They'd return to the
Appalachians briefly,
Soon as they could,
Often as they could!

Other country people
Didn't go so far,
Drifting into Asphalt Mountain,
Like Knoxville,

Hunting work paying
Wages
Which weren't
Skilled or union.

They'd come home
To the country
Every evening
Marginally surviving.

When closed doors shut
Out the city,
You could tell
They were back in the holler,

By how they talked, thought,
By what they wore,
By music they dialed,
By what was on the table.

2. VISITING FAMILY

The boy boarded the bus
With his daddy
Headed to say good bye
To his first cousin, who
Had a long trip
Ahead of him.
Uptown, cars crossed the
River. Guests departed the
Andrew Johnson Hotel, where
Hank Williams'd just died.

Man and boy entered the crowded
Hall where a mopper
Caused them to wend a way
Past a group
Standing, loitering, listening,
Watching his cousin
Talk, as friends, popped
In and out, doors
Clanged, echoed around the
Wide-eyed boy.

This family visit was special,
Made possible by the
County Building
Being uptown,
On the bus line on
Gay Street.
Both knew they wouldn't see
His daddy's nephew
Again for five
Years.

3. AFTERMATH

As a child he knew what
Adults thought of Roy.
They liked his mother who'd
Spent her life in a mill.
But he heard them say
Roy was a drunk,
Wouldn't hold a job,
Lived off his mother in the projects!
The boy liked Roy.
Roy'd sit on steps and
Tell him stories
About being a soldier in war,
About being bayoneted in the
Butt by a German.
Roy had time to talk to the boy.
As adult,
Like adults around him
When he was a child,
He had a different view of Roy.
War'd changed Roy.
The horror of being stabbed!
Cries, "Gas! Get your mask!"
Crouching in a trench in bombardment.
1918'd changed Roy.
For some the aftermath is worse
Than the war.
It goes on forever. There's no Armistice Day.

4. GONE TO EARLY

1958. The year they turned 16,
Living across the street from each other.
When school let out for the summer,
One walked out the door for the last time.

He spent summer in the country.
August, climbing a quarry wall,
He grasped a rock,
Pulling up, it fractured.

He fell, fractured rock on top.
Returning from football practice,
The other heard.
He couldn't believe it.

Crossing the street, he believed
When he saw his best friend
In the coffin.
It didn't look much like him.

Returning home in 1975,
His mother gave him an old newspaper
Article with friend's photo.
Framed, it stood on his desk 29 years.

When school let out each summer
Too many, too young,
Walked out the door
For the last time.

5. CITY DREAMS

Ulas came to the city from
Del-Rio with
Big dreams.
He got a job, married, bought
A house and
Raised a family.

Now grown old,
Their daughter and her family
Moved back to help.
Aged, Ulas still dreams,
Only now it's of
Del Rio.

His grandson called early,
"Grandpaw's dead, preacher.
Can you come?
Driving four blocks,
"He's in the back room.
Please close his eyes."

Using two fingers, he did.
Then watched them reappear.
Ulas returned to Del Rio,
Accompanied by the preacher.
Finishing the funeral,
Everybody left, except

Preacher and hearse driver,
Who removed jackets and ties,
Rolled up sleeves,
Shoveled clods of dirt and
Drove back to the city,
Where the big dreams are.

6. COMMUNION

Young preacher began taking
Communion
To those unable to attend worship.
After church'd shared Communion,
He'd visit homes and
Nursing homes, carrying
His small case.
For many it'd been so long
Since they'd experienced
Communion,
They wept openly.
After a visit in the County
Nursing Home,
Past the Work House, the
Church received a call,
A young patient wanted the
Pastor to visit.
Next time there, he dropped in,
And was astonished.
"Did you go to Rule High?"
"Yeah."
"I did too."
They knew each other from
Fifteen years back.
When they'd turned 16, and
School ended for the summer,
One walked out the
Door for the last time.
Swimming that summer, in the mountains,
He dove in,
Striking his head on a rock,
Emerging a quadriplegic.

He requested Communion.
Monthly visits continued
For two years.
Constricted physically,
His mind was free.
They talked openly,
Good for each other.

Kidney trouble began and
Worn out, he was ready to go.
Preacher accompanied him
Back of Newport and beyond,
To cemetery, top of the mountain,
Where he can see forever.

7. MORAL VALUES

Sitting in a church pew
Waiting
For the first Advent Service
To begin,
A friend handed him a
10 x 13 envelope, saying,
"That's for you."

Opening, he found an
8 x 10 newspaper photo,
Judging by the 2 year old boy
In the crowd,
It was probably dated 1990.
There a crowd waited for the
Community Market.

It's a heavily integrated crowd,
In the center is a much younger
Preacher and a younger friend.
They'd both graduated from
High School in 1960.
Preacher from all-white Rule.
Friend from all-black Austin,

They'd lived cheek to
Jowl in segregated
Communities,
Separated by the color
Barrier.
Then they learned
Better,

In the United States Army.
God bless that Baptist
Deacon,
President Harry Truman,
Who integrated the
United States Armed Forces
In 1948.

8. FAMILY VISITS

Preacher'd been to the
County Home
When he was little,
Visiting four of his
Cousins stuck there.

Every chance they got,
They'd run off to
Grandma's place,
Way out
In the country.

They'd stay
Until some people'd
Show up,
Collecting all four cousins
In a car,

Taking them back to the
County Home.
Growing up, preacher'd
Ranked County Home
Right there with Juvenile Hall.

His first year at the Center,
Lady resident asked
Him to visit her
12 year old boy at the
County Home.

Waiting, preacher was startled
Seeing her son walk up
Wearing a dress as punishment.
Preacher didn't know
What to say or do.

Shamed, hearing boy taunted,
Young preacher spent the
Next 29 years,
Learning, in increments,
How to help people.

9. COMMUNITY

Pleasant rain fell on the
Languid autumn morning.
Before it got busy, the
Preacher sat in porch chair
Enjoying cup of coffee.
Couldn't get much better.

Truck pulled up,
Discharging three
Painters for contractor,
To apartments across the street.
They'd lost a day's wages
In pleasant rain.

A single painter diverted,
Shaking hands on the porch,
"My name's Wylie.
I'm up from Chattanooga.
Met a lady over there
Two weeks ago."

Taking a seat
Tearing plastic bag,
Once holding a loaf of bread,
"Look here,
Taste my cooking."
It was the lunch he'd packed.

Barbecued pork tasted as
Good as it smelled.
Preacher brought another
Cup of coffee to the
Congeniality,
As rain gently fell.

10. TUESDAY'S CHILD

When school let out on Tuesdays,
Kids ran to Bible Club.
This Tuesday, preacher was
Caught off guard
When a Second Grader asked,
"What was Jesus' color?"
He told her,
"Come up here. Put your arm
Next to mine.
Jesus wasn't as dark
As your arm.
He wasn't as light colored
As my arm."
Deftly she asked,
"You mean Jesus was mixed?"

11. OUT OF THE MOUTHS OF BABES

Family moved into apartment
Just across the
Street from the Center.

Wasn't long before they discovered,
The Center was a
Welcoming place.

The mother visited Clothing Room
And Community Market.
Her boy joined Bible Club.

The mother told preacher's wife
What she heard her boy say,
When a friend asked,

"What do you do up
There at the
Center?"

"Well, on Tuesdays Tom tells
Us about Jesus.
On Thursdays we have fun."

12. FASHION CONSCIOUS

The 8 year old stumbled
Into Bible Club
In outsized LIZ CLAIBORNE shoes,
Pitiful on her.

What had other children
Said to her,
About her,
That day?

After the club meeting,
Shirley took her
Downstairs for a pair
Of tennis shoes.

Rather than the
NIKES, the
Girl set her heart on
A pair of sandals.

"Do you go to church?"
"Yes."
"Wear the sandals to church.
Wear the Nikes to school.

"Leave your old shoes, ok?"
" OK. If Mom gets mad.
I'll come back for them."
"No! Take them too."

13. HOW'S YOUR DAY?

2:30 P.M. Time for children,
Disgorged from school,
To rush in
For Bible Club.

Waiting staff counted
7 police cruisers
Across street at curb
And 1 paddy wagon.

Glancing left, they saw
A single lady, cuffed,
Being helped into the
Back seat of a cruiser.

Glancing right, they saw
A 1st Grade girl,
Tentatively walking
Up fence row,

Awed by armada of
Police Forces
Required
To cart her mother away.

14. SOMETHING MORE NEEDED?

School bell rang
Scattering children onto
City streets,
Leading 32 girls and boys
To the Center.

Janitor from Center
Met Josh
At his classroom door,
Walked with him up
To the Center.

Kids got bingo cards,
Tokens, and
Jackie whispered number
And letter to Josh,
Blind but not mute.

Josh'd shout information,
Kids squealing
With mounting tension,
Till Irene awarded
Prizes to winners.

Preacher sat on stage as
Children gathered on
Floor,
Listening to Bible story
In "Cotton Patch Gospels."

Following prayer,
They ran outside into
Playground,
Squealing, smelling
Hot dogs, chili.

Then they went
Home
To same peers,
Neighborhoods,
Family situations.

15. SEARCHING FOR LOVE

At 8 she'd rush to
Center after school,
Hugging, clinging to the
Staff.
When club was over
She walked slowly

Through Center's doors,
Through Projects,
To grandmother's apartment
Who raised
And loved
Her.

Rushing into marriage,
Then the
Horrible
Thing
Happened,
Reported on TV and in papers.

Hearing
Reading
Judge's sentence,
"51 years in prison
Before eligible
For parole."

Preacher could see her
Running through door.
He could imagine
Look on her face,
Fear in her heart,
When Judge's gavel fell.

He saw her grandmother's
Haggard face,
Standing in line in the
Community Market.
Lines in her face
More'n time warranted.

16. WHAT WAS SCHOOL LIKE TODAY?

Every eye in the classroom
Was on the clock,
Bell was about to ring.
Being winter,
They'd have to put coats on
Before rushing doors.

Just up hill from school,
Across street
From Center,
Similar tensions formed
When 3 police cars and
2 unmarked cars pulled up,

Belching 4 uniforms
And 4 civilians
To gather between
2 apartment buildings,
Then pursue a young man
Around the corner.

An officer caught him in middle
Of the street,
Putting him down,
Before bulging eyes
Of just released
Students,

Who ran into Center,
Telling staff,
"The policeman put his
Gun right on that man's
Head.
Did you see it?"

17. MEMORY VERSE

At weekly Bible Club
Children were encouraged to
Memorize
Bible verses.

This excitable youngster
Was new,
Making new friends,
Desperate to fit in.

When teacher asked,
"Who can say John 3:16?'
His hand shot up,
Waving.

Teacher thought
Perhaps he'd learned,
Riding one of church buses
Out of public housing.

His eyes danced,
His body shook,
When the teacher
Recognized him.

Innocently,
With huge grin,
He said
"John 3:16."

18.   THE DISAPPEARED

He was shocked to discover
Photos of
Missing children,
When two old film rolls
Were developed.

They were among the brightest
In the community.
They had parental encouragement,
And sought the Center's
Proffered assistance.

Their evaporation
Devastated hope.
Gone now
Were rising leaders,
Poised role models.

Their parents
Fled
Violence,
Drugs,
Schools.

19. PASSED INTO THE NIGHT

When the tutors drove up
From the university,
Kids were waiting outside,
Laughing.

Entering, spreading their
Homework,
Getting pencils, paper
Amid the laughter,

When the man walked in,
Scanning the crowd,
Belt looped in
His hand.

The preacher knew who he wanted.
"She's here.
Can't she stay
Till its over?"

"She wasn't supposed to come.
I'm watching her.
She come up here
Without telling me."

Hearing his voice,
She saw him,
Started crying,
And ran past him,

Passing into the night,
They heard,
"You can run,
But you can't hide."

20. THWARTED ONCE AGAIN

Two decades ago
In the Projects,
Excitement at Report
Card Day
Was artfully aroused.

Club kids darted
Through Center doors
On Report Card Day,
Flashing their work,
Demanding Laura mark it.

At the next Club Meeting,
All A's got $5.00.
A's and B's got $3.00.
Perfect Attendance
Got $1.00.

The morning following
Report Card Day,
Two sisters were waiting
When Laura arrived,
"Why aren't you in school?"

Dropping heads
Mumbled,
"We got head lice.
Moma needs our money
For medicine."

21. INFRACANINOPHILE

What a season.
They'd won it all,
The League Championship,
The Tournament Championship,
The Sportsmanship Award!

Transition was their forte,
Faster than their
Competitors,
Often faster than the
Referee's eyes.

The theme at
Ryan's Championship Dinner was,
No team had ever
Won it all before.
Trophies, photos went home,

A Church League Basketball
Championship
Didn't come any easier.
It cost sweat, practice,
Bearing the taunts of the N-word
After some games.

22. VISCERAL EXPERIENCES

The 15 year old strode
Through the door,
Ready for the hike in
The Smoky Mountains.

The staff cringed.
The last time he entered,
He ruined the hike for
Everybody.

Overruling his gut feeling
The leader was silent.
Everyone boarding the van
Was not excited.

Riding to the mountains
The kid leaned on a girl
Until finally
She switched seats.

On the hiking trail
He was constantly told,
"Hike your pants", and
Warned about remarks.

At the swimming hole,
He dunked others.
At the cook-out,
He took more food.

Returning home,
Weary hikers slept.
The kid
Threw food.

Viewing photos of the trip,
There was his wild water pleasure.
His enormous appetite.
His joy with others.

23. SUDDEN GORE

He was a kid,
Starting
High School.
Avoided trouble, studied.
Chose friends carefully.

Early that afternoon
He walked out the
Door,
A half block from apartments,
Heading to Convenience Store.

Just before he entered the
Store,
He heard angry, crisp
Words,
And turned

Watching bullets splatter the
Jacket of a young man,
Falling in the store's
Parking lot.

Stunned, he watched the police,
Heard the officer
Plead for a towel,
Or something,
To stem the flow of blood.

Everyone watched that scene
On the evening TV news.
The victim survived,
Nullifying newspaper's
Morning headline.

Will the gory scene
Vanish just
As easily
In the kid's
Mind?

24. SIDEWALK ART

Every time you passed
You were filled with
Anger and revulsion.

Didn't matter if raining,
Mid-day sun blasting,
Street-light illuminating,

Every time you passed
You were filled with
Anger and revulsion.

Chalk art work
Was featureless,
In yellow,

Every time you passed
You were filled with
Anger and revulsion.

Others passed with no
Reaction to
Art work's tale.

Whatever bike rider did,
Passing pick-up
Chased the bike,

Bumping over curb
Onto sidewalk,
Striking the bike.

Your anger's not directed
To sidewalk artist
From police department.

He traced outline of
10 year old
On sidewalk,

Using
Yellow chalk
Where he died.

25. EMMIT'S FIX-IT SHOP

Behind elementary school,
Facing
The Housing Project,
The Center was only
Service Station
For a long way.

Maintenance provided
Air for bicycle tires for
Kids across street.
A lady borrowed hammer
To straighten
Her car key.

This man borrowed bicycle
Pump for the
Flat on a neighbor's car,
So Housing Authority
Wouldn't pull her car.

6th Grade boy borrowed
Pliers
To fix chain on
His bike.
Working, head down,
He asked

"Can I add someone's name
To share my cabin
On my camp application,
If they live in
Another project
Across town?"

"You sure can.
Is he a friend who
Used to live
Here?"
"No.
He's my step-brother."

26. PICKING SIDES

Kids'd gathered at Center
After school,
Enjoying Movie Carnival,
When two policemen entering
Broke the enthrallment.

Moving out of sight
They asked if preacher'd consider
Letting people use the
Building after closing.
He knew where this lead.

It wasn't a 12 Step Program
In evening.
It wasn't mentoring for
Juvenile delinquents.
Location, Location, Location!

"Lot to see out front door,
Isn't there?"
Policeman laughed.
Preacher laughed.
"It's a great spot for

Standing in dark,
Watching out glass doors,
Observing
Illegal activity
Across street."

"It's a great way to
Serve Community,"
He mentioned they'd rather
Be trusted,
And approachable.

27. FLIGHT PATTERN

It was Tax Season and late.
Bill'd prepared returns for 31 tonight.
The last was a young man who'd
Grown up around the Center.
He asked if we needed help before
He left.

We were waiting for Bill to get
His paperwork together.
Before young man got to his car,
4 shots rang out down the hill.
Before we checked with Bill,
4 more shots rang out.

Our tax volunteer focused on
His forms and gear,
And didn't hear a thing.
When we asked what direction
He planned to leave,
"my cars pointing downhill."

The young man told him 8 shots'd
Been fired just a half-block
Down that hill,
"I'll make a u-turn and
Follow you out of here."

28. WHO'D BELIEVE IT?

Some volunteers' lives were
Bent
By their participation in
A single event.
They were a breed apart.

In 1984, there was Olga,
From Buda or was it Pest?
Her dad took the family to
Sarajevo, June, 1914.
Olga was in the city

When Archduke Ferdinand was
Assassinated and WWI
Began.
Today she teaches ceramics
To expectant girls.

In 1989 a Japanese-American told,
At age 12, she came out of Sunday
Mass at 8am, and watched
Zeros bomb ships on 7 December, 1941.
Today, she gives food to the poor.

June 6, 1994, the elder deacon,
When someone asked at 10 a.m.
"Where were you 50 years ago?"
Looked at his watch, saying,
"Three miles inside France."

He'd landed with the first wave
At Omaha Beach on D-Day.
Today, he gives food
And tells people how to
Cook eggplant.

29. CRACKLING FIRE

Among men some
Wax eloquently
On virtues
Of crackling fire.

Some woodsmen choose
To extol those woods
Which burn longest,
Heat fastest, most aromatically.

Others know
When to split wood,
How long to dry wood,
How to stack wood.

I've not encountered any
But I'm willing to
Wager
Some quibble over kindling.

Specialized knowledge
May enhance
Enjoyment of a
Crackling fire,

Especially when flames
Flicker on assortment of
Dried meats, homemade sausages
Chocolate and cheese fondues.

Yet one rainy night on
Front porch of
Center,
I immensely enjoyed,

Across the street,
A crackling fire, framed
By doors of a
Dempster Dumpster.

30. HE RESPECTS COARSE

Reading a poet describing Chicago,
The word that caught
His eye
Was coarse.
In 1958 he lost several
Friends.
Turning 16, they dropped out
Of school.
One went to Chicago and
Made a life.
Eighteen years later, he
Reappeared, asking
If they could talk.
School had just let out,
Center was full of kids,
So he asked his old friend
If he could hang around, or
Return in 90 minutes.
Whatever he had to say,
Died that evening
When he taped the garden hose
To his exhaust pipe.

31. SPEAKING IDIOMATICALLY

In the 70s, UT students came
Weekly to tutor children.
Message on one student's shirt
Caught preacher's eye,
"Have you Hugged a Pig Today?"

It made preacher think,
"Hey, this kid's proud of
His father."
Approaching, he asked student,
"Is your father a policeman?"

Student cocked his head quizzically.
Preacher quickly explained,
"Your shirt. Hug a pig.
Your dad's a cop,
Right?"

Student laughed,
"No. Pig, pig, pig.
I'm from Greene County,
A farmer in
Ag school."

32. A GOOD DEED GONE BAD

A Quaker group started it.
They gave the man a prisoner's name.
They meant good.
The man started writing the
Prisoner c/o Death Row.
He meant good.
Prisoner quickly wrote back.
He saw potential good.
Man wrote, mailed stamps, accepted
Collect calls, sent money and
Small gifts,
He meant good.
Prisoner requested a radio, even
Sent prison regs on how to
Send a radio.
He saw potential good.
Accepting collect calls in afternoon,
Man'd hear prison doors clanging,
Inmates shouting, radio playing,
His friend laughing.
He meant good.
It ended abruptly when
He read in newspaper,
His friend on Death Row
Turned his radio on,
And blast blew his head off.
Convicted serial killer'd
Used a prison made bomb.

33. AMBULANCE SHIFT

The teen rushed in,
Shouting,
"He shot himself, across the
Street.
He's laying in the yard!"

Preacher rushed out,
Crossed the street and
Found young man
Sitting up,
Bleeding from 2 wounds

In his head.
His mother rushed up,
Screaming
Crying
Bewildered.

Preacher got him up,
Got him to the van,
Laid him in the
Seat,
Told him to hang on.

Preacher helped his mother
Into van
And sped to
St. Mary's Emergency
Room.

34. DIEGO'S ARMORER

Despite his familiarity with a blade,
He was not a conquistador.
In 1993 he waded through the
Market Crowd,
"Tomas, a man wants to fight,
Saying I pushed him.
I don't want to hurt him.
Call the Police."
"There's the phone."
Pulling his shirt up,
Reaching into back of his pants,
Withdrawing a butcher and carving
Knife,
"Keep these for me."
His blades rested on Pantry shelf.
Police drove up and
Diego talked to them.
When they looked again,
He was in the back of the cruiser.
Later someone said Diego had
An outstanding warrant.
A month later he walked in,
Asking for his blades.
Nine years later, the phone rang
At home.
Diego'd been killed.
Preacher'd seen TV report on
A stabbing and death in
Alley behind station on Baxter.

Latino community confirmed
It was Diego.
There was no report or obituary
In the newspaper.
Like most of the conquistadors,
Diego's name is lost.

35. INTERMINABLE NOTICE

The 2 preachers'd
Walked, talked
On the track at
Malcolm-Martin Park
Behind Knoxville College.

Nearing end of the morning stroll,
They mentioned
The scattered colors
In the overgrown vacant lot
Across from the park,

Agreeing the artificial flowers
Marked the corner
Where a young man
Was shot and killed
Last week.

36. WHO KNOWS BEST?

He lived south
Of the river,
Secretly camped in woods
Off Chapman Highway.
Two, three times a week
He'd appear,
Clear across town,
Waiting until invited in.

Asked if he'd like
Lunch,
He'd sit on the porch,
Or in cold weather,
On choir seat
Inside the door and eat.
He'd read magazines
Till supper.

It'd poured all that day.
At closing,
He rode shotgun
Back toward town.
Asked where
He wanted to go,
"Take me to
Henley Street Bridge."

Down Cooper Street
Beside Old Gray Cemetery,
"Want out under the Inter-State,
Where its dry?"

"No. They won't let
Me stay.
Police'll arrest me
In 5 minutes."

Continuing up Depot, turning
South on Gay.
"What about letting you out
Across Gay Street Bridge,
Right in front of Baptist
Hospital?"
"Naw, if I don't catch a bus,
They'll make me leave,

"Turn here."
Driver followed directions.
"Let me out at the
church up at the Bridge.
They'll let me
Stay
Till it stops
Raining."

37. A GOOD NIGHT'S REST

Everybody's heard of
Couch potatoes,
Sedentary types,
Texting,
TVing,
Computering.

Have you heard of the
Couch population?
People staying with
Relatives, friends,
Sleeping on
Couch.

This debt to kin
Strains
Family relationships,
Food budgets,
Damages furniture,
Endangers tenants' home.

38. SCAVENGER HUNT

People coming to Community
Market for food, and
Clothing room for
Clothes, household goods,
Often brought something.

A couple proudly came
One morning,
Bringing a paper bag.
Jammed with
Them.

They'd chanced upon
Them,
Rummaging in dumpster,
Not far from their
Apartment.

Preacher opened bag to
Examine them,
Then caught a whiff.
Stench'd gag a
Maggot.

They'd have to sterilize the
Used eyeglasses,
Before shipping them to
The Christian
Medical Society in Texas,

Which'd send them to
Ecuador,
Honduras,
Nicaragua,
Costa Rica.

39. WHERE'S THIRD WORLD?

When he walked in,
He'd come to right place.
They almost didn't recognize
Him without his glasses, his
Faced marred by abrasions.

Sitting in old choir seat,
He told about his scrape,
Breaking his glasses.
He can't keep his job
If he can't see.

Finally he asked to browse in
Box of eyeglasses- those
Collected for Third World countries.
Shopping there before,
He'd known success.

This evening
He picked up pair after
Discarded pair,
Face distorting,
Then he whooped.

40. CUT YOUR NOSE OFF TO SPITE YOUR FACE

Monday a week ago,
Helen called the Center.
The night before, a young man
Knocked on her door,
Asking to use her phone.
He couldn't start his car and
Needed to call a friend.
She let him in.
After his call, he started talking.
"The next thing I knew
He hit me in the head 3 times.
I guess he thought he'd
Knock me out and get my purse.
I shouted, "Lord have mercy!
In the Name of Jesus!"
And he ran out the door.
Here I am with 40 stitches
In my head,
And my family's making me move."
I've watched her clean the
Parking lot, give rides all over
Town to people. She's the first
To call when something happens
At night.
Friday I watched her family
Pack and move her things.

41. TWO OUT OF THREE IS BAD

We met when he first ate
Supper.
During table talk I learned
He'd been out of
Eastern State and homeless
For five years.
Before I left table, he posed
This for instance,
"I know you can't give
Permission, but if a man
Slept on back porch tonight,
Would you call the Law?"

"You're right, I couldn't give
Permission, but if a man
Slept on back porch tonight,
I wouldn't call the Law."
That set temper of our relationship.
Charlie set the boundaries.
You'd never know when he'd
Drop in.
When he did, we'd sit and talk,
Overtime, I gathered he was
Dependent upon kindness of ladies
For shelter.

In time he aged enough to get his
Social Security Check,
And Senior Citizen's High Rise
Apartment.
His second month's rent wasn't

Due when
The phone rang.
A worker from his Senior Citizen's
High Rise informed me
Charlie had died, and my name
Was on his notification list.
Did I know how to contact his family?

42. CAREFUL WHAT YOU SAY

Like 213 others
That morning
She walked up to
Select food in the
Community Market.

Clad in jeans and a
Lace bra,
She prompted several
To ask preacher
To talk to her.

Preacher's wife went to
Clothing Room,
Emerging with lovely
Blouse,
Giving it on her entrance.

Picking food in Community
Market,
Blouse was not on her back,
She carried it
In her hand.

Preacher asked her to
Don blouse,
She replied,
"I was told it don't matter
What you wear to church."

43. CAREFUL WHAT YOU ASK FOR

Top and the preacher found a corner.
Top'd been in Bastogne, Dec. 1944,
With the 101st Airborne.
Later jumps left him with an
Artificial leg.

Preacher's wife came up from hot,
Crowded Clothing Room
And found their corner.
Exasperated over a man who'd
Insulted and threatened others,

She blurted, "If I had a gun,
I'd shoot him."
Reaching into his front pocket,
Top pulled his 32 cal. Pistol,
"Want to borrow mine?"

She blanched and walked off
"Preacher, I'm too old to fight.
I can't outrun anybody.
But I ain't gonna let
Somebody just beat on me."

44. MINISTRY OF BIRTHDAYS

Felix was a Native American
From Minnesota.
How he got there they
Never learned.
He lived in a second story
Apartment,
Across the street.

One evening eating supper,
Felix was loud, his
Distraught eyes welling with tears,
"I know I'm going to
Die in that apartment
Over there.
I've had AIDS two years.

"I can't keep food
Down anymore.
I only weigh 100 pounds.
It was my fault.
I used a dirty needle.
I'll be 36 on August 17.
It's all a waste."

August 17, you should've seen
Felix blow out his
Birthday cake candles.
Beneath a Felix the Cat poster,
He cried opening gifts.
He cried again when
They sang HAPPY BIRTHDAY.

45. PROJECT VFW

Food Pantry had closed
When an old friend pulled up.
He lives in a nearby project,
Always ready to talk.

He'd served with a scout dog
Detachment in Viet-Nam,
Spending a lot of time in the field,
Exposed to Agent Orange.

He frequently visits
VA,
A long way down the Inter-State
In West Knoxville.

He'd been to VA today.
They gave him
An injection
Despite him being alone and driving.

Army lingo calls it
Extenuating, mitigating circumstances.
It earned him an
Unofficial generous bag.

46. A HELPING HAND

That morning
A cold rain
Pelted the crowd
Waiting for
The Community Market
To open.

143 families
Trudged through,
Without reciting their
Name or address,
Or revealing
Why they needed help.

Their presence spoke for them.
Last one through
Was a crippled
Man.
Laboriously he made
His selections.

Laboriously he crossed the street
To an old clunker,
Placing his selections
In the back seat,
And talking to his companion
In the front seat.

Laboriously he traced
His path
Back across the street
In the pelting rain,
Standing soaked,
He had one plea,

"Can I get food
For my friend?
He's in a wheelchair.
Both of us'll be soaked,
Getting the wheelchair out,
Pushing him over and back."

47. BUSTED

A way station appeared
On the corner,
Sporting a couch and
2 kitchen chairs,
For friends of a friend
Confined by AIDS.

It mushroomed and the
New occupants were soon
Doing a brisk drug
Business,
And they and their clients
Soon trashed the corner.

The Center cleaned it up,
And the preacher
Put it off limits.
When 2 unsavory characters
Stood on the corner,
Preacher told them to leave.

Before he got back to Center,
A new car squealed to a stop,
Right in front,
A suit jumped out,
Flashed a badge,
"They're undercover,"

Just as a kid bicycled by,
Looking at the 2 on the corner,
Pedaling furiously
Into the Projects,
"Five O,
Five O's on the corner!"

48. SIDEWALK HYPOTHERMIA

Three remembered, A fourth revived.
Verlin was troubled,
His home was a car, jacked up,
Wheels removed, outside the
Beer joint, across from the Projects.
His body was found one winter
Behind stores in the strip mall.

Pete was cantankerous.
He lived in a deserted block store,
Devoid of heat and water.
He'd lost several toes to
Frost bite and used crutches.
His body was found one winter
Behind a neighborhood market.

Kenny was a tush hog, feared by
Students and faculty, until he
Dropped out when he was 16.
His last trek was driving a
Mid-Way to Mexico.
His body was found one winter
Uptown on Gay Street's sidewalk.

A cold evening, after closing,
People left clothes on the porch.
A volunteer came early,
Noticing the clothes moving, and
A hand emerging.
Billy was almost frozen.
She took him home to warm him.

Charity warmed Billy, but
<u>The Backpacker's Field Manual</u>
 Says,
"The key to combating
Hypothermia is
Prevention."

49. STRIKE 3, YOU'RE OUT

It's not a game.
We're talking about
Life here.

In the 80's
Burgeoning prison populations
Were Society's answer to ills.

Commit 3 felonies,
Receive Habitual Criminal label,
Bear a life sentence.

He was 25 years old
When the judge's gavel fell
With his new label.

When Society couldn't afford
Harsh long sentences,
Habituals were released.

Preacher and ex-con met,
When ex-con was 45
Doing community service,

Singing for his lunch,
"I put the gold band on the
Right left hand this time."

50. BUY BUST

Truck's cab held a
Couple
Who coasted to a stop
In front of the Center.

They sat, smoked, waited
Til a young man
Crossed the street, parking
His arms in the cab window.

A hand emerged from the cab
Holding something,
Taken by the young man, who
Returned across the street.

Was it a drug deal
On Center property?
The couple's faces, wore
Big grins,

Greeting 3 unmarked vehicles,
Blocking the street,
Disgorging 11 undercover
Cops,

Chasing and bringing to the
Ground, the
Double crossed young
Man.

51. AFTERMATH

He was wizened, living alone.
They'd noticed him in the Community
Market, bearing welts, bruises.
That led the preacher into the
Banking business.
Instead of getting drunk and being
Robbed of all his money,
He'd give the preacher most of
His check, and make
Weekly withdrawals.
That worked.
Getting food, he asked one day
"Tommy, do you know what DSC is?
"The Distinguished Service Cross?
Second only to the Medal of Honor?"
"I'll bring mine up sometime
and show you."
His citation praised his
Extraordinary heroism
Under enemy machine gun and
Rifle fire. He killed 14
Enemy soldiers, saving the lives
Of the men in his platoon in
April, 1945.
When he drank alone
He"d call the preacher at home
At night
Different hours, different nights,
But always the same question,
"Tommy, do you think
God'll forgive me?"

For some the aftermath is worse
Than the war.
It goes on forever,
There's no V- J Day.

52. UNWITTING ENFORCEMENT

The Community Market at
The Center
Was calling in
The unnamed,
The unaddressed,
The unquestioned,
One at a time.

Two police cruisers
Parked
Half block shy of
The Center,
Discharging two officers,
Ticketing two
Parked cars.

Shirley was calling
Numbered people
Into the market, and
Noticed a dozen or
So people
Didn't enter when their
Number was called.

Aloud, she said
"Where is everybody?
What's happened?"
A voice in the waiting crowd,
"Probably had outstanding
warrants.
Police scared 'em off."

53. CLEVER EVASION

Back three years,
The young man'd vanished
From the face of the
Earth,

After being shot in
The chest
To balance his
Drug debts.

Entering the Center,
Preacher was surprised
To see who was
Waiting for him.

Preacher remembered
Visiting
Every hospital in town
Searching for him.

Hearing the fruitless efforts,
The young man wore a wry smile,
"I used my daddy's last name,
So nobody could find me."

54. DETECTIVE SKILLS REQUIRED

Walking through the Projects
The preacher saw
A common scene.

Someone's furniture, possessions were
Unceremoniously stacked
Between sidewalk and curb.

He knew the lady
Evicted,
Then saw her mother

Standing nearby
Selling stuff to get what
She could for her baby.

Another resident told
Why she was
Evicted.

She let a felon live in her
Apartment,
Breaking Housing rules.

"You can't tell by looking
At a person's face, if
They're a felon."

55. HIDDEN TALENT

Crowd breakfasting AL FRESCO at
The center's café
Was swollen by Community Market
And Clothing Room visitors.

Bail-bondsmen cut a swathe to
A breakfast patron,
Grabbing his shoulders to
Apprehend him.

He escaped their hold,
Leaving them with his jacket.
He dashed off the porch,
Down the side steps,

Hurtled the fence,
Sped across a neighbor's yard,
Vaulted their fence,
Lunging into captor's arms,

Pinning him on the street,
Pummeling him into
Submission. Watching, the
Preacher recalled his basketball prowess.

56. OBLITERATED

Rain cleanses streets and sidewalks
In the Projects.
Blood was spilt last night
On the sidewalk.
There was nothing in the media about
A knife fight.
There was nothing in the media about
Someone stabbed.
Blood on the sidewalk says there
Was a fight,
And somebody was hurt.
Do we wait for rain?
A housing authority worker,
Carrying a bucket and a broom,
Washes the blood away.
Soon it'll look as if it rained.

57. COMMUNITY LIFE

Delivering the monthly newspaper
In five Projects,
Two doors had signs.
One read:
    DON'T ASK TO USE MY PHONE.
    PEOPLE THINK I'M A DRUG DEALER
    WHEN SO MANY PEOPLE
    USE MY PHONE.
Second one read:
    DON'T COME HERE BUMIN.
    BRING BACK WHAT YOU'VE
    BUMED FROM US
    AND MAYBE WE'LL HAVE
    SOMETHING YOU CAN
    BUM FROM US.

58. PUNISHMENT OUGHT TO FIT THE CRIME

Visiting the Jail
Was like old Home Week
For the preacher.
Somebody from high school
Or the projects'd
Hail him.

A voice from a recess
In the wall,
A voice secluded
From the others,
A hoarse voice,
Called out.

Edging closer to the
Bars,
The preacher
Peered in,
Not knowing the voice,
Nor the skeletal apparition

Telling him
His name.
The preacher couldn't
Believe it.
He was a shadow of
His former self.

Another inmate hailed the
Preacher and told him
Their friend'd been
Repeatedly raped.
He'd stopped eating.
Was isolated now.

Preacher called a
Chaplain at
Eastern State Hospital,
Who got him out,
Transferred for
Observation and care.

What had he done?
The state said
There was a
Reason
He was in jail.
He bought a hot TV.

59. LAMB AMONG WOLVES

Newspaper's murder story
Was flat.
A homeless man released
From jail on a
Public intoxication charge,
Was found beaten to death,
A week later,
Under the viaduct on
Woodland Avenue and I-275.

They'd gone to
High school together.
Like so many before him,
When he turned 16,
He went out the
School doors
That summer
For the
Last time.

When they recognized
Each other
At the Center,
He became frequent guest,
Always helping
Carry out trash,
Police the yard and street,
Clean restrooms.

Helping set up
Badminton and Croquet
Courts for kids
After school one day,
He said,
"It's a bad day.
I'm 49 today."
When the preacher returned,
He was gone.

60. DATING SERVICE

The eighteen wheeler pulling
Up out front,
Air brakes whoosing,
Excited everybody.

The driver strolled in,
Asking
If we'd like 300 pair of
Cowboy boots.

"Yeah,"
Imaging 300
Cowboys
Line dancing in Public Housing.

Smiling,
We signed tax form.
Grabbed huge boxes
And began unloading

Unloading
Unloading
Unloading
Unloading.

Carrying boxes in,
Dragging them downstairs,
Through the hall,
Engorging the room.

The driver winked,
Drove out of sight,
As we sought
Mates,

To no avail.
We possessed
600 singles
Seeking mates.

61. WASTED TALENT

It all started
With no fanfare or siren,
When a lithe figure,
In a single motion,
Opened the apartment door,
Leaped over concrete
Porch,
Landing in dirt.

The athletic figure grabbed
The porch stanchion,
Muscling up atop the
Porch roof, where
His CONS confidently
Ran up the
Sloop of roof to the spine,
Which he strode,
Balanced by out-stretched arms.

Gathered crowd's
Voices encouraged
His venture to second story
Roof's spine,
Which his glide across
Mocked tightrope walker's.
We all stood rooted,
Rooting the lithe figure's
Dangerous flight.

Was it honed skill or
Athletic ability
Which won the day?
He descended to the ground
Safely,
Till his pursuers
Blocked his escape route.
He sits alone, in the back seat,
On a project street.

62. ESCORT SERVICE

It was quiet at the Center
When he
Saw her
Distraught,
With reason.

Preacher'd read newspaper
Report about the
Police searching for
One of her
Boys,

A suspect in the
Shooting and
Killing of another.
A drug deal
Gone sour.

She blurted,
"The police
Shot at him
Last night
On the East Side.

He's at my place now.
My husband
Talked to him
All night.
He's ready to

Turn himself in.
He's scared of running,
Afraid the police'll
Corner him and
Shoot him.

My husband sent me
Up here to ask you
To take him,
And my son to the
County Jail.

He wants you to go
In with them,
When he turns himself in."
Preacher jumped in the van
And drove to her apartment.

Her husband and a friend
From AA
Came out before the
Young man and his girlfriend
Furtively snuck out.

Parking uptown in
First Baptist Church's
Parking lot,
All 5 walked to the
City-County Building.

5 people had to knock
At 3 places
Before
The young man
Could turn himself in.

Jail personnel were
Pleasant, friendly.
They found the warrant and
Told the family what was
To happen.

The police escorted the young man out.
Her husband said to the preacher,
"You see how he looks.
Not beat up.
He's going quietly."

63. DEFIANT PRESERVATION

Pulling up to work, they found
A couch, 2 chairs, end table
And ottoman
On the porch, in the rain.
Soiled, tattered, drenched,
Fit only for the dump.
A pick-up stopped, a couple
And a man got out.
As the couple examine the furniture,
The man siddled over,
"A friend dropped my furniture off.
It's for sale ."
Then we heard, "this is not what
We're looking for."
Later, the owner emerged out of an
Apartment, "I'm selling it to get
Gas to leave town. If I can't, its yours."
"Man, you've got to do something quick.
There's going to be a crowd here soon,
And we're going to need this space.
This is in bad shape, and the rains
Not helping."
The young man never flinched. "You got a knife?
I want to see if I left money in the couch."
Handing him his pocketknife,
The silence was overpowering.
The only sound was the ripping of fabric.
Even the rain fell silently.
The young man worked swiftly, silent himself.

Next time he looked,
The porch was deserted,
Every piece defaced and his knife
On the end table, folded.

64. DOES ANYONE CARE

Preacher can still see him,
Head, upper body
Out the window,
High on paint.

He's yelling, laughing,
Preacher hears his name.
The rest is undecipherable.
Silver paint rings his lips.

Rooms behind him
Are empty,
No longer filled
By family.

He died soon after,
Alone,
In an alley,
Troubled, haunted.

Apartments were raised
59 years ago.
And razed
59 years later.

Now, he's not.
Neither is his window,
Building, buildings,
Sidewalks, streets.

65. THE PISTOL WAS ON THE TABLE

Right where he put it
Before he sat down.
It was between us, closer to him,
Right where he put it
Before I sat down.
Distraught, he wanted to talk.
I listened.
The phone rang,
Someone said it was for me.
I took the call,
Standing in the hall.
Catching movement, a glance
Revealed him listening.
We re-entered and the pistol
Was back on the table,
Right where he put it
Before he sat down.
It was between us, closer to him,
Right where he put it
Before I sat down.
I listened.
5 minutes later, 2 uniformed
Police officers entered.
He grabbed the pistol.
Out 4 eyeballs riveted,
"You listened. I didn't mention
The police."
The police talked to a staff
Member, and left.
The pistol was back on the table,
Right where he put it,
Before he sat down.

It was between us, closer to him,
Right where he put it
Before I sat down.
I listened,
Then I took him home.

66. PARKING ATTENDANT

The car'd been parked on their corner
For almost a month.
He knew why.
His first car was a 1950 two-door
Maroon Plymouth,
Passenger floorboard rusted out.
Every time it rained hard,
Flathead engine's spark plug wells
Flooded.
Frequent vapor locks, despite wooden
Clothespins lining gas line, common.
At UT he'd park headed downhill
So he could jump-start it.
Yeah, he knew why that car'd been
Parked on their corner,
And he knew why it was stranded
On their corner.
Housing Authority'd tag a car if
It sits too long in their
Lot or on their street,
And then haul if off.
They waited until a resident came over,
Saying master cylinder was busted
On her car,
And she finally had the money to pay
Somebody to fix it.

67. SUMMER PLACE

Every autumn,
Leaves drifting down
Reveal a vacant summer home,

Defined by outdoor
Furniture,
A fire pit in a grassy area.

Spring sprouted leaves
Curtain the summer home
From prying eyes, and

Shelter and protect the
Homeless atop the
Salvaged platform in the tree.

68. HANGING ON

There must've been a knock
For him to open the door.
Whoever it was,
Threw lighter fluid
On him, and
Flicked a BIC.

Lurid details
Dominated
Conversations
At the church.
The preacher
Remembered the hanger-on.

Preacher'd been asked
To do Bible Study
At nearby nursing home.
He intuited the patients
More'n likely'd appreciate
Stronger gifts.

Sure enough,
In subsequent weeks,
Several elderly folk'd
Drowse
During his
Soliloquy.

Standing back,
He'd witness a
Resurrection.
That hanger-on who normally
Picked and sang to a younger
Crowd at local clubs'd

Belt out old
Gospel favorites,
Accompanied by
Ancient foot tapping and
Clapping
All over the hall.

69. WHO RATTED THEM OUT?

There were few successes.
He was one.
A young man raised by a
Single mother
And older sisters.

Discipling himself in
The weight room,
He developed muscular prowess.
A volunteer helped
Him gain a good job.

The night he heard
A sister's husband'd
Repeatedly struck her,
He went hunting.
He ended drinking.

Arrested Friday night,
He sobered up in jail,
Then called,
"Can you bail me out?
I got to be at work Monday.

There's a crazy man in here.
The fool's pulled a knife on me.
I'll get your money next week."
He said,
"All I got's a check."

"You got to bring money.
They won't take a check."
Not having that kind of cash,
He called his uncle at the
Insurance office,

Getting a $100.00 loan.
He went to City Jail
To post bond.
The jailer went to the tank
Yelling the young man's name.

"Somebody's paid your bail."
When young man stood in the tank,
The jailer stared,
"Sit down.
That ain't your daddy out there,"

70. A PLACE FOR YOUR PILLOW

A piece of paper on the
Door
Said it.
A glance inside, through
A window,
Confirmed it.

Official looking document
Labeled
"Writ of Possession",
Flooded
His mind,
With questions.

Who'd lived here?
How long before it got to this?
Could anybody've helped?
Where are they now?
Where do you go
When you're kicked out of the projects?

71. DUPLICITY

When asked,
His crippled body
Shrouded, in mystery,
A car wreck?
A beating? A fall?

Verlin never told
The same story twice
In a row.
He rather enjoyed
Questions.

His last skirmish
With the law
Netted more'n 11-29.
Verlin spent 3 years
In Brushy.

Returning to town,
He dropped by to see the
Old preacher,
His friend now
Over 2 decades.

He'd huffed paint
2 decades and more,
Saying 3 years in
The pen
Cleaned him up.

Hugging, preacher caught whiff
Of metallic spray paint.
He did what he
Always did.
Hugged him harder.

72. MIRRORED RESPONSE

A summer in the mid 90's,
He walked into
The center.
He and the preacher'd
See each other in the
Development and nod.

He used to work for the
Housing Authority,
But had some
Troubles.
Preacher'd heard he'd
Become a Muslim.

This was his first visit,
And he studied the
Pictures of Harriet Tubman,
Sojourner Truth,
And the bust of
Martin Luther King, Jr.

He was surprised and
Delighted
To spot the youth football picture,
Pointing to himself on
The back row of
Coaches.

He told the preacher
He used the Holy Bible
And the Holy Qur'an
To reach young men
Before they leave the streets
Sentenced to prison.

Sitting at the table,
Talking, sharing concerns,
The two men had a
Lot more in common
Since he'd become
A Muslim.

73. ALONE TOGETHER

This morning, in a drizzling rain,
She strode down the street,
Alone,
Carrying two valises.
The evening before, she watched,
Alone,
As workmen from the Housing Authority
Gingerly piled her belongings
Between the sidewalk
And the curb. She sat,
Alone,
All night, on her furniture and clothes,
In the rain,
Until the police and the truck arrived
This morning to haul it all away.
There's been a spate of
Evictions this week,
And others have witnessed their
Belongings gingerly piled
Between the sidewalk and curb.
Alone, together,
They've all walked away.

74. AUTUMN ON THE HILL

On the hill
Sandwiched between Vermont and Maryland
Avenues,
Rule High School's stadium
Raised hopes of gridiron glory.

The stadium's full of ghosts now.
Rule's been closed over
Two decades.
Projects across the street've
Been demolished.

No Friday Night Lights.
No High School Rivalries.
No Players Warming Up Without Pads.
No Union of Black-White Parents Cheering.
Only Razed Hopes of Gridiron Glory.

75. RETURNING HOME

Yeah, the preacher
Remembered,
He'd baptized all 3.
He went back a long way
With them.

His daddy'd worked
At the plant
With their grandpa.
He'd played high school
Ball with their uncle.

He remembered
Their funerals too.
The first,
The oldest,
Was a motorcycle wreck.

At the graveside,
A brother sat a
Boombox blaring
LYNYRD SKYNYRD'S
"Free Bird."

Next funeral was occasioned
By one pulling a
Cain and Able kind of thing
With a knife.
What could be said?

Third brother
Died of natural causes,
In the penitentiary.
There's wasn't a
Funeral.

76. POVERTY RESTRICTS EXCESS

At Christmas
Every child got presents,
Except a quiet
Ten year old girl.

She remained missing
When her gifts
Were taken
To her empty apartment.

When school resumed,
She reappeared.
Asked if she'd had
A good Christmas,

She reported,
"I got my bike fixed."
Then her gifts
Were unwrapped.

77. CHANCES ARE

He's eight years old.
Penetrating eyes.
Yesterday they sat
On the front porch
Talking,
Before the man returned
His hammer.

The night of the big
Christmas Party,
Waiting on the same front porch
For the buses to
Carry them away,
He'd banged, banged, banged
Till his hammer was confiscated.

A teenager shared his story,
Others chimed in,
"He's pitiful.
All he sees are
Drunks, prostitutes,
Funny men.
They all treat him like
He's a lot older."
They know already.

78. TRAPPINGS OF POVERTY

The week after Christmas,
Looking out the kitchen window
She saw a little boy sitting
On the ball field.
He tried to get up, but couldn't

Bernado picked him and his
Old girl's bicycle up,
And brought them inside.
Cold and hurting he'd been tackled,
Fell on his hip and heard it pop.

He lived across the street, so
Bernado went for his parents.
He got his 15 year old brother.
His parents were at the
Blood bank.

She called to speak to the parents,
But confidentiality prevented it.
When she told what'd happened,
She got his mother,
Who couldn't come.

They'd pulled in on empty, and
Had to donate blood to get money
To buy gas.
So she told her we'd take him to
St. Mary's, and wait for them.

A nurse placed him in a wheelchair.
Do you take any medicine? Ritalin.
Do you take it once a day? Three times.
Have you had breakfast? Up at the Center.
He slept some.

She spoke gently and untied his sneakers.
Anguished, "Don't take off my shoes."
He had no sock over his dirty foot.
"I just want to check your pulse."
2 hours later, his parents came in.

79. IMAGINE

New faces appear in the Community
Market all the time.
Some speak in unknown tongues,
Ukrainian. Spanish.
Romanian.
At Christmas, sure the
New couple was Latino, he said
"Feliz Navidad e prospero anno."

When the lady gave him a
Blank stare,
He repeated,
"Feliz Navidad e prospero anno."
In broken English,
Her husband interjected,
"We don't speak Spanish."
"Where're you from?"

"Guatemala."
Huh?
Guatemalans speak Spanish.
Then it hit him.
History's the same throughout the Americas.
"You're Indian?"
He nodded, "yes".
"What language do you speak?"
Being the newcomer, he didn't comprehend.

80. SAVING THE BEST FOR LAST

That morning,
He'll not forget that
February morning
When he heard
The news.

Hazel had been
Found,
Dead,
In her front yard
That morning.

Her death was
Natural,
No violence,
Her heart gave out.
She dropped dead.

The Christmas just
Passed
Was when she got
Her first
SSI check.

Following the impulse of
Her worn out
Heart,
She crossed the Inter-State
To Star Sales.

Using her back
Pay, she
Bought 3 boxes of
Toys for the
Center to pass out.

81. VENTURING OUT

In 2 weeks, Christmas 1990'd
Be here.
Teens at Center were excited.
Their annual holiday excursion
Was going to Gatlinburg.

Most had never been and
None had been during
Winter,
Seeing the lights
And snow.

Walking, slipping in, out
Open shop
Doors,
Teens held McDonald's
Ice cream, shakes.

Adults hugged steaming coffee,
Hot chocolate.
Sugarland's Visitor Center lawn
Hosted snowmen
And snowball fights.

Tired, gift laden, packed into van,
They returned
Down Chapman Highway,
Over Henley Street Bridge,
To Knoxville.

Nearing the apartments,
Dropping off one or two
At a time,
A lady crossed to their side
In headlight beams.

Standing in light, waving,
Hustling-for drugs or
For kids' presents?
All saw her. None spoke.
They knew they were back home.

82. LOCATION, LOCATION, LOCATION

Vernon walked in,
Jittery, excited and sat down.
"Me and 3 other guys were standing
By a dumpster
On Bonnyman.

"Two police cars squealed up,
cops jumped out,
put their Glocks on us,
And told us
Not to move.

They checked our ID and for
Outstanding warrants.
They were looking for burglars,
But we didn't fit their
Descriptions.

They had their Glocks on us, Tom.
I ain't shot.
I ain't spending Christmas
In jail.
I just thank God."

83. ON THE THIRD DAY OF CHRISTMAS

A lady entered the Center,
Laden with wrapped gifts
And a basket of food
For a family across the street.

She'd carried Christmas
Gifts and food
To their apartment where
No one answered the door.

She left a note for
The family's mother,
Saying gifts and food
Waited for her at the Center.

The next day
Nothing was heard from
The family.
A phone call was unanswered.

On the third day,
A staff member crossed the street,
Knocked, and
Looked in the window.

The apartment was stripped
Bare.
In the middle of the room stood
An artificial Christmas tree.

84. WINTER SOLSTICE

Joe and Mary lived in
Big Springs
Just south of Decatur.
Joe couldn't find carpenter work,
Except part-time construction.

When he heard there was
Work in Knoxville,
He and Mary, 9 months pregnant,
Got in the pick-up
And headed up I-75 north.

Getting to Knoxville late,
There was no room at
Motel 6 or Red Roof,
Lights flashed, NO VACANCY
Clerks said it was the holidays.

They asked a policeman if
He knew where they could stay.
He told them to follow
His blue lights.
He took them to VOA on 5th Avenue.

They'd no more'n got into the room
When contractions started.

85. CHRISTMAS IN THE INNER-CITY

She was Christmas shopping at
K-Mart on Broadway
When she got mugged.
Feeling a pull on her purse strap,
She turned and was face to face
With a young man.
He knocked her cart over,
Pushing her over it and down
Onto the parking lot wet asphalt.
He ran with her purse
To a waiting car,
Which turned out of the lot,
North on Broadway.
She got up screaming.
Clerks took her back into K-Mart
And called the Police.
Sitting, soaked by rain puddles,
Suffering bruises and scratches,
A young lady approached
Carrying her purse,
Saying she found it behind K-Mart.
It was dry, clean, and had all her cash.
Nothing gone,
Except a packet of photos.
When her husband and son arrived,
She was calm.
After Christmas, several young people
Heard her story at the Center.
One said,
"That sounds like Mack. He writes script
And steals credit cards."
She didn't know who they were

Describing.
Her husband did.
Mack'd grown up in the clubs,
Camps and activities,
And last summer he came in to
Use the phone,
And posed for a photo.
When he showed it to her,
"That's him. He's the one."
She never told.
He never returned.

86. NON-BREAKING AND ENTERING

Everybody was downstairs except
The janitor.
Called, he went down for 60 seconds.
Coming back up he met the kid
Coming out of the office,
Saying his mother sent clothes and
He was looking for someone.

When Shirley came up she found
Her billfold half out of her purse
In the office,
And $75.00 was missing.
The janitor told her about the kid
And she went to his
Apartment.

When the preacher came in,
He found
A policeman talking to the kid,
"I didn't take nothing,"
and his mother,
"A bunch of kids could've gone in there."
The officer walked away on the phone.

That's when the preacher lit in,
Talking about the Center,
His moma crying,
His little brother and sister
Sitting there scared, and
Him going to Juvenile tonight,
And he owned up to it.

Told to go get the money,
The kid went out the door just
As the officer returned.
They came back in, the
Kid cuffed.
"Tell your mother where it is,
She can go get it.

The officer removed the cuffs,
Saying, "There's been a shooting."
When his mother returned,
She gave the money to Shirley,
And the kid asked to speak to us.
"I've been to counseling for stealing.
Moma couldn't buy Air Jordan's,
So I took your money."

We hugged him. He left.

87. PUSHED TO THE LIMIT

When moma left for Bible Study at the Center,
Daddy didn't lock the door.
Arthritic old man, bent, slowed,
Went to the back yard.

The culprit came up the steps,
Tried the door, called out,
And was rifling dresser drawers
When daddy walked in.

Culprit grabbed a chair
Took the old man's wallet,
Telling him he'd kill him
If he had to.

Nervous, hurrying, unsuccessful,
Watching the old man watching
And fearing he'd go to the
Closet where the pistol was.

"Give me the basement key."
That's when daddy said,
"No. Its time for you to leave.
You're in enough trouble already."

He left, making daddy go to
The front porch too.
"Stay here till I'm gone."
Running down into the projects.

Rheumatoid Arthritis stole
Daddy's movement,
The perpetrator stole his pride.
Together, they left him enraged.

88. GIVE TILL IT HURTS

Sunday, moma was at church
Just up the street,
She and a neighbor sat
Near the back.
When the pastor called for
Altar Prayer,
They went up front to pray.
In the back, another preyed.
Returning to their seats,
Their purses were gone.
Four months later,
Moma got a call from
Across town,
Asking if she'd lost her purse,
"Yes."
The caller said,
"Someone found your billfold
On the sidewalk and
Turned it in.
There was no money or credit cards
Or a purse."
Sister took moma to get it.

89. BLACK RIBBONS

An old country custom,
Immortalized by George Jones,
"He stopped loving her today,
They hung a wreath upon his door,"

Accompanied country people's
Immigration to the city.
He remembers, as a boy, seeing wreaths
On doors where death visited.

Today, nobody'd dare announce
Death, and its attendant
Funeral and burial absences,
With a black ribboned wreath,

Just like addresses
Disappeared
From obituaries
Declaring funeral, burial times.

When his daddy
Died in 1987,
In the sad house across the
Street from the projects,

People broke in twice.
Once, the family found it ransacked,
And then a neighbor
Drove off an intruder.

90. MISSIONS REBOUND

Tentacles of poverty'd
Writhed
Last few days.
Walking into the Center early
He found the break-in.
All day long he showed the evidence.

Earlier a man was killed
In the apartments
Without an obituary marker.
At 1 a.m. a sniper'd fired
At a car, blocks from the Center
At I-275 exit.

Mid-day they heard a 16 year old
Birthed after 29 hours labor and
A "C" Section. Parents are school drop-outs.
That afternoon,
A lady here for the Food Pantry,
Had a son in jail

Charged in the stabbing death of a
Lady who frequented their
Mid-Week Worship.
She resisted over
$12.00
To feed his drug habit.

Later, a lady, her 3 children,
And a friend walked in for
Community Kitchen Supper.
Not long ago her friend
Inappropriately touched a youngster
In the Mid-Week Worship.

This evening a Christian brother
From Nigeria came to
Eat supper;
A student at UT until ill.
Preacher walked him around
Repeating his angry litany.

"Look what they did there.
Look at that door,
Smashed to smithereens.
We've been here 16 years.
This is the first
Break-in we've had!"

Richard smiled.
"Tom, God is saying,
'I've protected you for 16 years.
Now you've had a bad day,
And you're ready to return
To Egypt?'"

91. AFTERMATH

John served in 'Nam in '69 with 1st Cav.
Got home. Had 2 months to pull,
So went home. He was tired.
He got a BCD with no VA benefits.
He'd lived in an apartment with his
Mother and sister, till they died.
He lives alone now.
In line, you notice black hair to shoulders,
Black beard down to chest.
They shared war stories.
He was proud of his awards, folded in
His shirt.
The preacher was proud he unfolded them
A couple of times to show him.
Told he's been baptized by a chaplain in
"Nam, in a rice paddy, his unit drawing fire.
He soon joined up.
Downstairs, the ladies love John.
He'd eat lunch with the staff and get
Paid in kind:
Set of dishes, a chair, a winter coat.
On week-ends preacher'd drop him off
With a little cash.
He had liver and kidney trouble and was found
Dead, in his chair, TV flashing.
They buried a hero in Potter's Field,
Near the old Work House.
For some the aftermath's
Worse than the war.
It goes on forever.
There's no Paris Peace Talks.

92. WORD OF COMFORT

The phone rang
In the middle of the night.
By 1:30 a.m., he was outside the Center,
Watching smoke roil out
The front doors.

Lights on top of 6 fire trucks and
2 emergency vehicles
lit the sky.
Firemen and hoses covered
The grounds.

When morning came,
Volunteers secured demolished windows
With sheets of plywood.
Electricians restored power and saved
Food in freezers and refrigerators.

Temporary lights were set
Up downstairs,
Doors torn apart by firemen were
Secured. Plumbers replaced ruptured
Lines and restored water.

Insurance claims adjusters interviewed staff.
Arson investigators, ATF Agents all
Told them a Molotov cocktail was
Thrown through a
Downstairs window.

TV reporters clamored for interviews.
Preacher never said a word.
All the next week volunteers
Swarmed. Phone calls and letters were
A part of each day's routine,
An inmate wrote from prison:
"There are several of us guys up here
who apreshaate the things
you have done thru out the years.
I know the fire broke Sherlie
Hart and I can emagin what it
Done to yours. I want minnite no
Name of us, but when the persons are
Caught we would like to know their
Names as soon as possible.
Yes, you know us all."

93. CAUTION

A stranger ignored the
Poster's warning,
At 1:14 AM Thursday,
Hurling a Molotov cocktail
Through a downstairs window,
In direct violation of the
Poster's warning.
The poster rests tonight,
Scorched yellow and black,
Bearing a ribbon.
Scorching almost obliterates
The old warning,
    NO SMOKING
The bright, yellow ribbon
Barks a new warning,
    CRIME SCENE
    DO NOT ENTER

94. CERTIFIED

Yesterday a young couple
Entered the Center,
Asking for the pastor.
Introducing himself,
They shook hands all around.
The couple asked to speak
In private.

Mid-Week Worship'd
Just ended.
The crowd gathered at
The Fellowship table.
The quietest place
Around was the
Stairwell.

Shutting the door, into the quiet,
The couple told the pastor
God'd impressed them to
Come up and
Pray for him,
"We have a word from the Lord
For you.

Some of it you won't understand,
But God wants to
Strengthen you.
Can we pray with you?"
Joining hands, forming a circle,
She began
To pray for the pastor and ministry.

Her prayer increased in strength
Till she spoke in tongues,
Soon joined by her
Companion.
Then she pulled a vial
Out of her purse,
Anointing the pastor's forehead.

Having completed
God's instructions,
The couple left as
Quietly as they'd
Come,
Never to return in the pastor's
Last 14 years of ministry.

95. IS THIS HOW'S IT'S SUPPOSED TO BE?

December 2. 8 AM.
28 degrees.
She stood at somebody's driveway,
Near the intersection of
Two neighborhood arteries.
Between her and the
Elementary school
Was a house.

You came down the street,
Slowing for the STOP sign,
Seeing you, she turned,
Looking directly into your
Eyes,
And smiled.
An encouraging smile?
A despairing smile?

96. IS IT SAFE?

A mother called from Mississippi,
Worried about her college daughter,
Spending the summer at the Center.
She read the papers, watched news
About crack, and red and blue colors.
It's not your normal summer camp.

Every Monday a van of teens'd escape,
To the Smokies' trails,
Checking bear scat, ground churned by
Wild hogs, deer tracks,
Verdant horizons.
Monday, June 28, 1993, was fateful.

Buildings receded and images of Alum Cave,
Chimney's Picnic area,
Swimming holes, grilling hamburgers,
And a late return home
Filled eager minds.

Topping Arch Rock, tormented by
Torrential rain,
Crossing Styx Creek, and
Stopping only 50 yards from a
Dry creek bed, they turned back.

The next morning's newspaper reported
A cloud burst at 6:30 PM'd
Sent a 20 foot high flash flood
Careening down that dry creek bed,
Scouring vegetation to the bed rock,
Depositing large trees and boulders.

97. MASKED

Closed up. Locked up. The day over.
He dropped a friend at his apartment,
Turned onto main artery through the Projects,
And stopped.

Cars going and coming
Were blocked by a car going,
Now standing, full of young men,
Surrounded by young men,

Standing in the middle of the street,
Some leaning on the car.
He recognized several
Former members of Center's Clubs,

Who'd served a period as success stories,
Holding paper bags revealing
Bottles of malt.
Their stance and disinterested glances at

Stalled motorists,
Challenged anyone to honk.
No horns blared.
Nobody was in a hurry.

Stoic masks masked what?

98. TREASURED HEIRLOOM

Over 200 families were in line for food.
Amidst the melee a lady shouted,
"Tom, that picture there- of Kathy.
I'll give you $5.00 for it."
The entrance hallway has large
Picture frames holding photos of
Children and adults,
Spanning generations.
She pointed at the photo of a little girl
Last summer in Vacation Bible School.
With mock surprise, he asked,
"Why do you want my picture?"
Tears welled in her eyes, her chin quivered,
And she said,
"They took my kids. I don't
Have a picture of her."
Moving close, he told her,
"Look how busy it is. Come back when
The crowds are gone, or wait and I'll
Give you her picture."
When the crowd dissipated, he took
The frame down, removed her picture,
And laid it on his desk.
There it remained,
Until he retired 5 ½ years later.

99. WHAT IS REQUIRED?

The Baptist and the Methodist
Spent their lunch hours
Walking.
Today, they walked Oldham Avenue,
Which cuts a swathe
Through two hills,
Dotted with public housing.
The earthly possessions of two families
Had been carefully
Removed and deposited
Between curb and sidewalk,
On Oldham.
People had rifled others'
Property, strewing remains.'
Climbing to the crest of one hill,
Standing on Virginia Avenue,
Where the Baptist'd grown up,
The Methodist said,
"Standing here I can see for miles.
There's downtown Knoxville, the
Sunsphere, Ayers Hall,
Even the Smoky Mountains
But the cluster of apartment buildings
In front of me,
Blocks my view of Oldham Avenue,
I'd have to intentionally go down there
To see the suffering.

100. HIDDEN FROM VIEW

This morning at the
4- way STOP,
The old man appraised
Again the
Old house.

At this same spot,
As a little boy,
A forest of oaks
Hid the
Old home.

When he was 8,
Government saws
Hewed the towering oaks,
Exposing the
Old house.

At 10, he watched
The oaks replaced by
Concrete block public housing,
Blotting out the
Old house

Almost 6 decades later,
The government
Razed the projects,
Revealing the
Old house.

Not for long.
The porch has caved in.
The sides are dappled with age.
Sheets of plywood shroud windows,
Like the old man.

ABOUT THE AUTHOR

Tom Everett was born in Knoxville, Tennessee in 1942. Following graduation from the University of Tennessee (1964), he served five years as an officer in the Army, including a year in the Dominican Crisis (1965-66). He received a Master's Degree from Southwestern Baptist Theological Seminary in Texas (1971). After pastoring three and a half years, Tom and his wife Shirley were appointed Home Missionaries, serving in inner-city Knoxville (1975-2004). Mr. Everett received two Fellowships (Spring Term, 1999; Spring Term, 2004) at Harvard Divinity School. Tom and Shirley live in Knoxville. They have two children, Susan and Matthew, and a granddaughter, Riley.

27135978R00089

Made in the USA
Charleston, SC
02 March 2014